THE COMPOSITE GUIDE

IN THIS SERIES

Auto Racing

Baseball

Basketball

Football

Golf

Hockey

Lacrosse

Soccer

Tennis

Track and Field

Wrestling

THE COMPOSITE GUIDE

to **SOCCER**

JOHN F. WUKOVITS

CHELSEA HOUSE PUBLISHERS

Philadelphia

Produced by Choptank Syndicate, Inc.

Editor and Picture Researcher: Norman L. Macht
Production Coordinator and Editorial Assistant: Mary E. Hull
Design and Production: Lisa Hochstein
Cover Illustrator: Cliff Spohn
Cover Design: Keith Trego
Art Direction: Sara Davis

First Printing

1 3 5 7 9 8 6 4 2

Library of Congress Cataloging-in-Publication Data

Wukovits, John F., 1944-
    The composite guide to soccer / John F. Wukovits.
        p.   cm.— (The composite guide)
    Summary: Traces the history of soccer, from its beginnings, to its
first stars and championship games, to the notable players of today.
    Includes bibliographical references (p.) and index.
    ISBN 0-7910-4718-0 (hc)
    1. Soccer—History—Juvenile literature.
    2. Soccer players—Juvenile literature.
    [1. Soccer.] I. Title. II. Series.
    GV942.5.W85   1998
    796.334— dc21
                                                                98-14296
                                                                     CIP
                                                                      AC

CONTENTS

PELÉ

The man who was universally acclaimed as the greatest soccer player in the world—Pelé—stared dejectedly at the crowd of reporters as they scribbled his words in their notebooks. The 1966 World Cup, the World Series of soccer, had just ended amid controversy. The referees had permitted so much rough play throughout the tournament that limping players became a common sight. Pelé had been so viciously targeted by opponents that he missed the second game due to injuries. When he returned for the third contest, the Portuguese team seemed to be purposely trying to hurt the Brazilian star and force him out of the match.

His national team had been knocked out of the World Cup in three games, and Pelé angrily attributed the poor showing to violence. In a blunt, crisp tone he told the reporters, "For me there will be no more World Cups. Soccer has been distorted by violence and destructive tactics. I don't want to end up an invalid."

However, before the next World Cup in 1970, soccer officials ordered the referees to put an end to the rough tactics, which threatened not only Pelé but the other popular athletes in the sport. If any player engaged in dirty maneuvers, referees intended to flash a yellow card as one warning, then a red card for ejection if the unnecessary roughness continued.

Brazilian star Pelé, left, uses his head to knock the ball six yards for Brazil's first score in their 4–1 win over Italy for the 1970 World Cup championship.

Pelé was only 21 when he led Brazil's team to their second consecutive World Cup victory in 1962.

While reassuring to Pelé, the game's greatest player had already decided to participate in the World Cup. He could no more remove himself from the game than a fish could take itself out of water. He loved soccer and could not sit out while his Brazilian teammates entered the fray. As he explained, "It's the only thing I ever wanted to do."

Pelé, whose real name is Edson Arantes do Nascimento, received his love for soccer from his father, who Pelé claimed "was the greatest soccer player who ever lived. He just never got a chance to show everyone." Though his father may have been talented, the youngster showed that he would easily surpass him in soccer, for he amazed onlookers with his talent. Playing the position of striker, he showed that he could kick as hard and accurately as anyone, that he could outrace defenders even though he had to dribble the ball with his feet while he ran, and that he could outleap anybody else. Some observers claimed that Pelé could soar almost six feet in the air, then deflect the ball toward the goal with his head.

As a result, Pelé started his professional career in 1956 with the Santos, Brazil, squad at the tender age of 15. By the time of the 1966 World Cup, he was earning $2 million a year and was the most famous athlete in the world.

The Brazilian team members arrived at the site of the 1970 World Cup games in Mexico City unsure of their chances. In 1958 a young Pelé had scored two goals in the decisive game to lead Brazil to its first World Cup championship. Four years later he sat out the final game with an injury as his teammates rallied to capture a seond consecutive title. Now, in

1970, Brazil hoped to be the first nation to bring home three World Cup championships. With the aggressive style of play flashed by stars such as Pelé, Tostao, Jairzinho, and Carlos Alberto, many observers considered Brazil among the pre-tournament favorites.

They were placed in the same division with the defending champions, England, who boasted such a potent lineup that most onlookers marked them as the team to beat. Bobby Moore led a superb offense that contained many of the same stars from four years earlier. If the opponents swooped in on goal, the English could count on their world-class goalie, Gordon Banks, to rescue them with a dramatic save.

"We never thought we would get past the first round," explained Brazilian striker Rivelino. However, with Pelé showing flashes of brilliance and other team members stepping to the front, Brazil swept past every opponent with relative ease—except England—and put on such a strong display of offensive soccer that one account labeled the 1970 World Cup as "perhaps the best ever to be staged."

The Brazilian team gained confidence with a convincing 4–1 victory over Czechoslovakia. While Pelé scored one goal and set up others for teammates with accurate passes, he sent spectators home buzzing with a memorable shot that barely missed going in. From just inside his own half he spotted the Czechoslovakian goalkeeper straying a bit far from his goal. Pelé launched a powerful kick and watched as the ball soared high into the air, then plummeted behind a startled goalkeeper. Realizing he was hopelessly out of position, the goaltender watched in shock as the ball neared the goal, then bounced just inches from going in.

The second game, considered a classic by most observers, pitted the Brazilian team against the defending champions from England. Immediately, spectators knew that they were viewing soccer at its best, as first one side and then the other dashed to the attack, advancing toward their opponent's goal with razor-sharp passes and speedy feet.

Fans rose from their seats at one juncture in the game, fully expecting to see the great Pelé score. Jairzinho rushed the English goal from the right and somehow lofted the ball toward Pelé, who soared in one of his patented vaults to direct the ball with his head toward the goal. Gordon Banks, who had been covering the right side of the goal to block an expected Jairzinho shot, was caught badly out of position, but he somehow threw himself

Even the greatest get their share of bruises. Here Pelé takes a tumble in an NASL game in New York.

across the goal mouth and twisted upward to deflect Pelé's almost-certain goal up and over the crossbar. An incredulous Pelé stared with open eyes at the save which most accounts call "the best seen."

Brazil defeated England, 1–0, and won their next three games to reach the finals against Italy. Playing before more than 112,000 fans in the stadium and a worldwide television audience of one billion, Pelé opened the scoring by jumping high over his defender, twisting in midair, and heading the ball past the stunned Italian goalkeeper. Though Italy squared the match at 1–1, Brazil kept the play in the Italian end of the field and swarmed all over the enemy net. With Pelé dishing out splendid passes to his teammates, the Brazilians won an easy 4–1 victory.

With this victory, Pelé became the first player to perform on three World Cup champion teams. In leading Brazil to the win, Pelé's combination of accurate passes, amazing shots, and selfless play were the epitome of soccer at its best.

Off the field, he served as the game's perfect ambassador, signing autographs and talking freely with press and fans alike.

As a result, Pelé served as the ideal role model for youth around the world. He helped transfer the excitement and drama of soccer to young boys and girls, who then became the next generation of soccer enthusiasts. "Pelé's example, both on and off the field," claimed a public relations expert, "has been one of the factors in their love of the game."

蹴鞠戯　ケマリアソビ

2   FURY AND VIOLENCE

Although many nations claim to have originated the game that developed into soccer, most historians agree that the earliest version occurred in ancient China. In 1697 B.C. the emperor, Huang-Ti, formulated a game called tsu-chu that was played with a leather ball stuffed with cork and hair. The game relied mainly on the feet for propulsion. One thousand years later the Japanese followed with kemari, and a North African group called the Berbers devised a game in conjunction with their crops. Using the head of a sacrificed animal as the ball, two teams contested for the honor of burying the animal's head in their fields, thereby ensuring a bountiful yield.

The game spread to Europe with the ancient Greek game called episkiros, which allowed the kicking and tossing of a ball within set boundary lines. The Romans then borrowed the Greek game and turned it into harpastum, a contest that was hugely popular among Roman soldiers. The Roman legionnaires took the game with them to whichever portion of the empire they were stationed in; within a few years an early form of soccer appeared in many parts of Europe.

One place adopted the game introduced by Roman soldiers and fashioned it into their own. English citizens, nobility and peasantry alike, quickly developed a fondness for the rough-and-tumble athletic contests introduced by Rome

This ancient Japanese woodcut shows a game of kemari, a forerunner of modern soccer.

during its occupation between A.D. 43 and 407. Legend states that a talented squad from the town of Derby challenged their occupiers to a game, then soundly defeated the startled Romans.

The first appearance in writing of the English form of soccer occurred in 1175, when an English monk mentioned a game called ludus pilae. After using the head of an animal for a ball in contests which served a purpose similar to the Berber fertility rites, the English switched to animal bladders filled with air, and eventually to leather-covered balls. The game also transformed from a contest over town fields to the simple concept of having all the men and boys from one village battling the men and boys from another. In this riotous game, which frequently degenerated into a raucous series of fistfights, villages could have as many players as they wanted, and the winning side was whichever team kicked the ball into their opponent's village. By game's end the countryside was usually littered with the gasping bodies of players moaning from broken bones and blood-drenched faces.

Ludus pilae permitted almost anything, but it gradually came to be called football because it was played on foot, rather than on horseback. Since players did not need a horse, which only the wealthy could afford, soccer took hold with the common people. Most country villages soon had their own team of men and young boys kicking, tossing, and running with a ball.

The game moved into England's larger cities, where crowds of boisterous men rampaged through the streets, kicking a ball and thrashing

This scene of soccer football as it was played in the streets of London in the 14th century shows why King Henry II banned the sport in 1314.

into each other. People started to decry the violence which inevitably accompanied any football contest. The games turned so brutal that one 16th century diplomat, Sir Thomas Elyot, wrote that football was "nothing but beastly fury, and extreme violence, whereof procedeth hurt, and consequently rancour and malice do remain with them that be wounded."

Another leading writer of the day, Phillip Stubbs, condemned the sport as a "bloody and murdering practise" in which "sometimes their necks are broken, sometimes their backs, sometimes their legs, sometimes their arms, sometime one part thrust out of joynt, sometime their eyes start out." He added that as a result, the games were filled with "hatred, displeasure, enmity, and what not else, and sometimes murder, fighting, brawling, contortion, quarrel kicking, homicide, and great effusion of blood."

Consequently, a series of royal edicts restricted or forbade football. On April 13, 1314, Edward II banned football: "For as much as there is great noise in the city caused by hustling over large balls from which many evils might arise which God forbid; we command and forbid on behalf of the King, on pain of imprisonment, such a game to be used in the city in the future."

His successor, Edward III, did likewise, but for a different reason—the game affected the efficiency of his soldiers. Upset that his archers, whom he needed in battle against France and other enemies, were playing football rather than practicing their archery, Edward dispatched sheriffs to stop "such idle practices." He warned that an unpleasant prison sentence awaited any of his soldiers who wasted time playing "skittles, quoits, fives, football or other foolish games which are no use."

Richard II extended the ban in 1389 to "tenise, football and other games," while

A 16th century drawing depicts an early form of soccer played in an enclosed area.

James III of Scotland focused on two sports in his 1457 law, which ordered that "footballe and golfe be utterly cryed down and not to be used." Queen Elizabeth I hoped to protect her main city, London, in 1572 by issuing a law proclaiming that "no foteballe play be used or suffered within the city of London and the liberties thereof upon pain of imprisonment."

Despite these royal edicts, the game flourished throughout the English countryside, where teams from rival villages would play to determine area champions. A few rules started to define the game's nature, although they varied from place to place. Distances between opposing goals were shortened to a half-mile, then to a shorter range. Other rules attempted to limit football's violence.

In the early 1800s the game spread to English schools. Though the rules were not uniform throughout the country, most schools agreed that the ball should be advanced mainly by foot and that the use of hands should never be permitted. However, some schools preferred playing a game in which a player could pick up the ball and run with it. Thus two forms of football emerged from English schools. From one, rugby would develop. From the other would come football, or as it is commonly called in the United States, soccer.

3

NO TRIPPING
OR HACKING

Avid football enthusiasts started organizing the game in 1848 when a group from Cambridge University in England compiled a set of rules. They hoped to accomplish two tasks: to differentiate football from rugby, which permitted the use of hands, and place more emphasis upon skill rather than violence. Especially galling was the alarming incidence of kicking one's opponent, called shinning or hacking. One man muttered angrily that "the players kick each others' shins without the least ceremony, and some of them are overthrown at the hazard of their limbs."

Fourteen years later a man named J. C. Thring published a shortened version of these Cambridge rules. One edict, clearly designed to distinguish football from rugby, stated, "Hands may be used only to stop a ball and place it on the ground before the feet." A second rule admonished, "Kicks must be aimed only at the ball" instead of at your opponent.

In 1863 representatives from 11 English football clubs met in London and formed the London Football Association. Their rules included: "Neither tripping nor hacking shall be allowed, and no player shall use his hands to hold or push an adversary." The date on which these rules were issued, December 8, 1863, is accepted by many to be the birthdate of football, now known as soccer.

One branch of soccer grew into rugby, a rough game that allows players to pick up the ball and run with it as well as kick and pass it.

Apparently arising from student slang, the word "soccer" combined an abbreviated form of "Association"—meaning those who played by the London Football Association rules—with the "er" ending. Though the word football is used today in most parts of the world, the United States uses soccer to distinguish it from American football.

Eight years after the London Football Association issued its rules, the organization sponsored its first Challenge Cup tournament to decide a national champion. In 1872 the first game between two national teams occurred in Glasgow when the English national team met a team from Scotland. The competition was popular from its inception, and in 1882, 73 teams from all parts of England entered

Scottish players added a new dimension to soccer. Whereas the English focused upon advancing the ball by foot, called dribbling, Scottish athletes complemented this with a passing attack. This emphasis upon teamwork led to a higher caliber of play, and before long Scottish teams dominated soccer in Great Britain. Between 1876 and 1885, the Scots defeated the English in eight of nine contests.

Professionalism arrived in the sport during the 1880s when Scottish teams began paying men to play for them. The practice soon spread to other parts of Great Britain, and by 1888 twelve professional teams had been organized into the Football League—the world's first professional soccer league.

Around 1870 German teams started using the Football Association rules. Other portions of Europe followed closely behind. In an effort to control its far-flung empire, the British government stationed soldiers in many different countries. As their Roman predecessors had done centuries earlier, British soldiers introduced soccer wherever they served.

The inhabitants of South American nations became so enamored with soccer that fans of one country equated a victory over a rival nation with a triumph of war. Conversely, a defeat was seen as a national disgrace. Heated emotions frequently led to riots following games, and in some places armed police officers patroled the grounds to ensure order, while moats or even barbed-wire fences shielded players from angry spectators. During one

South American fans get very excited at soccer games, no matter who is playing. An Argentine soccer official holds a chicken that hit him when fans threw all kinds of things onto the field.

World Cup Final, Argentine fans, in a display that could hardly have been reassuring to Argentine players, erupted in the cheer "Victory or death!" As proof that soccer had truly caught on in the continent, 51,000 fans watched Uruguay defeat Switzerland for the gold medal in the 1924 Olympics.

To keep up with world demand and to better organize the sport, seven nations sent representatives to a 1904 meeting that formed the Federation Internationale de Football Association (FIFA). The organization remains the worldwide governing body of soccer.

Under the dynamic leadership of Jules Rimet, the Frenchman who headed FIFA 1921–54, soccer became the number one sport in the world.

In the 1920s the Olympics banned professional athletes, so Rimet and Henri Delaunay established the World Cup games. Surpassing baseball's World Series in popularity, the World Cup is held every four years. Teams representing each nation compete in various sectional tournaments to determine the final 22 teams, plus the host team and the defending champion, that will clash in the actual World Cup event.

Thirteen nations participated in the initial World Cup tournament in 1930. Since Uruguay had performed so well in the Olympics and the nation was celebrating its 100th year of independence, Rimet selected that South American nation to host the event, a decision that angered many European nations who felt they deserved the honor. Only four European nations—Belgium, Yugoslavia, Romania, and France—sent teams to Uruguay.

Other problems plagued the first World Cup. Miserable officiating enraged coaches and players. In one match the referee awarded five penalty kicks, while another referee officiated with such a loose hand that opposing players practically attacked each other with impunity. Police had to quell a riot during the Argentina-Chile contest, and a referee halted play six minutes before he should have just as France was about to tie its match with Argentina. When Uruguay defeated Argentina 4–2 in the Final, raucous Uruguayan fans took to the streets in a mad display of joy, and each player received a new home for his efforts. In Argentina, however, upset fans pelted the Uruguayan embassy with rocks.

In spite of the problems, soccer had been firmly planted in South America and other parts of the world. Even the one major nation that resisted soccer's appeal—the United States—shared the limelight in 1930 by scoring the first goal ever tallied in the World Cup and unexpectedly winning two games. However, their dreams of taking the inaugural trophy dissipated when the pre-tournament favorite, Argentina, trounced them in the semifinal game, 6–1.

Viewed by more spectators around the world than any other competition, the World Cup has exceeded the dreams of even such staunch advocates as founders Rimet and Delaunay. In 1994 the United States hosted the international competition for the first time amid hopes that the sport would carve out a niche in the sports-hungry nation.

GREAT GAMES AND PLAYERS

4

Modern soccer has entertained people for over 130 years. Dramatic goals, exhilarating saves, and heartbreaking losses have taken fans on such a roller-coaster ride of emotions that by game's end, each spectator feels physically and mentally spent. Epic matches and memorable athletes grace the pages of its history from its infancy until the present. Two such games stand out from its earliest days—the 1950 World Cup match between England and the United States, and the 1966 World Cup Final that pitted mighty England against a powerful West German squad.

The English soccer team traveled to Brazil for the 1950 World Cup confident of showing that they deserved the appellation handed them by their Italian colleagues—i maestri (the masters). Experts pegged them, along with host Brazil, as the tournament favorites, mainly because of superb dribbler Stanley Matthews and forward Tom Finney, possibly the best all-around player ever to don an English uniform. Above all, the English intended to put in their place all the other national teams that laid claim to the same title. The modern game had originated in England, and it was time to show the rest of the soccer world how the game should be played.

In one of the most stunning upsets in soccer history, however, on June 29, 1950, the English were defeated by a ragtag group of amateur athletes from a nation that could hardly boast

British soccer legend Sir Stanley Matthews is carried off the field by Russia's greatest goalie, Lev Yashin (left) and Madrid forward Ferenc Puskas after the 50-year-old Mathews' last professional match in 1965.

an organized soccer program. The 1950 United States team was not only unknown to the soccer world, but was unrecognized in its own country. Counting among its ranks an undertaker, a carpenter, a teacher, two mailmen, a machinist, an interior decorator, and a factory worker, the athletes had played only two games together as a unit before arriving in Brazil. One of the players, defender Harry Keough, explained, "We were just a bunch of amateurs playing against a bunch of professionals and nobody on our team had the wildest hope that we would beat England."

England put tremendous pressure on the Americans from the game's opening minute. They continuously pressed into the American half of the field and unleashed booming shots. One glanced off the crossbar; another smacked into the post. Above all, though, superb goaltending by Frank Borghi kept the English from scoring.

Eight minutes before halftime the unexpected occurred. Right halfback Walter Bahr smacked a shot from 25 yards out. As the English goaltender, Bert Williams, rushed over to block it, Joe Gaetjens headed the ball past the startled Williams for a 1–0 American lead. Though clearly a goal, the English players berated Gaetjens and claimed it was nothing more than a lucky deflection from a player who was trying to duck out of the way.

Though embarrassed by the goal, the English remained confident that with more than another half to play they would handily win the game. They applied steady pressure for the rest of the first half, and intensified their wild play as the minutes wound down in the second half. However, they could not dent the American defense. Borghi, playing the game of his life, turned aside every shot and led his team to a 1-0 upset over mighty England.

Neither team advanced beyond their next game. A disheartened English squad fell to Spain, 1–0, while the Americans were outclassed by Chile, 5–2. Despite being knocked from the tournament, the American coach Bill Jeffrey hoped the victory over England would reap dividends back home. "This is all we need to make the game go over in the States," Jeffrey stated. Unfortunately, his comment proved premature.

"We shall win," boldly declared the manager of the English national team, Alf Ramsey, shortly before play opened in the 1966 World Cup. He had a right to be confident, for he could field a superb defense and three of soccer's great players—goalkeeper Gordon Banks, center back Bobby Moore, and offensive wiz Bobby Charlton.

West Germany centered its attack around soccer's newest star, halfback Franz Beckenbauer. In a controversial move, however, the West German coach restricted Beckenbauer's immense ability to advance the ball and score by assigning him the task of marking, or defending, Bobby Charlton. The coach hoped that Beckenbauer would neutralize Charlton and limit the English squad's penchant for scoring.

Before 100,000 rabid fans at London's Wembley Stadium and 400 million watching on television, the two teams floated back and forth on the field for 13 minutes. The West Germans seized the lead when they capitalized on a failed English attempt to clear the ball. Ramon Wilson headed the ball to his West German teammate, Helmut Haller, who powered it by a screened Gordon Banks for a 1-0 lead.

England knotted the contest six minutes later when Bobby Moore escaped from Beckenbauer's shadow and propelled the ball deep into the West German end of the field before the defenders had a chance to set up. Geoff Hurst caught up to the ball and headed it by West German goalkeeper Hans Tilkowski.

Both teams pressed their attacks, but fantastic saves by Gordon Banks and Hans Tilkowski prevented any further scoring until the second half, when Martin Peters tallied with 12 minutes remaining. Delirious English fans rocked venerable Wembley Stadium with their cheers. All the English team had to do

Halfback Franz Becken-bauer starred for West Germany in the 1960s. Here he dribbles between two opponents while playing for the New York Cosmos of the NASL in 1978.

was hold on for a short time and the World Cup would be theirs.

They almost made it. With only 15 seconds left, the West Germans received a free kick near the English goal. Banks and his teammates formed a wall to deflect the expected shot. While 100,000 people in the stands held their breath, a West German winger powered the ball toward the goal, but the English successfully deflected it away. To their dismay, however, the ball bounced directly to another West German who knocked the ball into the net for the tying score. The two teams headed for overtime.

The aroused English took the lead when Geoff Hurst steered a pass from Alan Ball that hit the underside of the West German crossbar, bounced down, and spun away from the goal. Immediately, the English claimed the ball had crossed the goal line while West Germans argued just as vehemently that it had not. As the huge crowd again lapsed into nervous silence, referee Gottfried Dienst consulted with the Soviet lineman, then announced that the ball had crossed into the goal. England led, 2–1.

When Hurst added another goal in the overtime's final minute, he not only secured the World Cup for England but also became the first player in World Cup history to score three goals in the Final. English fans could now happily support their claim that they owned the best team in the world.

As with any sport, soccer has had its share of superstars. In its earlier years, four men stood out for their stellar play: Stanley Matthews, Lev Yashin, Gordon Banks, and Eusebio.

Called the "Wizard of Dribble" for his agility in skirting defenders and passing the ball, England's Stanley Matthews electrified audiences for over 30 years. Born in 1915, he started his professional career at age 19 in a game against Italy and did not retire from first-division soccer until five days after his 50th birthday. In 1956 he received the first European Footballer of the Year award, and in 1965 he became the first soccer player to be knighted.

His amazing body control, which enabled him to trick a defender into moving one way while he dashed the other, matched his legendary ball control. A noted writer once gushed of Matthews, "At his feet, the ball was at home, comfortably nestling in absolute security, caressed with soft little touches as Stan shuffled his bowed legs toward yet another hapless fullback."

Matthews so dominated play that a portion of one game has actually gone down in history as the "Stanley Matthews Minute." With his team trailing 3-2 with under three minutes remaining, Matthews single-handedly spun the opposing team in circles while he delivered precise passes to teammates for two quick scores. As a sportswriter summarized, the crowd erupted in joy "for the man who had turned the game around, who had treated us all to one of soccer's greatest games."

Fellow Englishman Gordon Banks and Lev Yashin of Russia form possibly the finest duo of goalkeepers ever to play the sport. Born in 1937, Banks spent hours practicing his game and studying film of himself, other goalies, and his opponents. During games he frequently talked to himself to charge up his emotions, and he moved about the goal with such grace that people said a lead for his team was "as safe as the Banks of England." When he stopped what seemed to be a certain goal from the foot of Pelé during a 1970 World Cup game, the Brazilian could only shake his head in wonder and call the save "impossible."

Sadly, Banks lost his right eye in a serious 1972 automobile accident. Though he returned to the game, Banks was never the same player and soon retired.

Born eight years before Banks, Lev Yashin played his entire professional career—over 600 games—with Dynamo Moscow, the team he joined in 1953. He first achieved fame during the 1956 Olympics, when the Soviet Union captured the gold medal, but added luster with superb performances throughout the 1950s and 1960s, during which he led his team to five Russian championships.

Yashin, so friendly that he was popular with teammates and foes, loved to roam from his goal and challenge opposing players. Called "The Man in Black" because he liked to wear black when playing, Yashin was named the 1963 European Footballer of the Year, and received his nation's Red Banner of Labor medal in 1957, and the Order of Lenin Medal in 1960. The talented goalkeeper retired in 1971, shortly before 100,000 grateful fans showered the athlete with acclaim at a game held in his honor in Moscow.

The first world-class soccer star from Africa, Eusebio powered the ball with the ferocity of a missile and tallied goals at an alarming pace. Born in Mozambique in 1942,

Born in Mozambique, Eusebio starred for Portugal in the 1960s. Here he heads the ball during an attack on England's goal in a 2–1 loss during the 1966 World Cup semifinals.

Eusebio grew up amid poverty with his seven brothers and sisters. He so loved the game as a youth that he played barefoot until he located a single soccer boot in a garbage dump. He carried that boot with him until he signed a lucrative professional contract with Benfica of Lisbon, Portugal, at age 19 and received a new pair.

He alerted the soccer world to his talent with one of his first games, a contest between Benfica and a team of Brazilians led by Pelé. When Brazil jumped out to a huge 5–0 lead. Benfica's coach sent in the young athlete to see what he could do. In less than 30 minutes

Eusebio smashed three goals into Brazil's net. In subsequent years he led Benfica to 10 Portuguese championships and the 1962 European Cup.

Eusebio scored goals at an unmatched pace. During the 1966 World Cup tournament he notched nine goals to lead all scorers, and he stood atop the Portuguese league in scoring every year from 1964 to 1973. Eusebio ended his professional career by playing in North America in the 1970s, where he helped win a championship for Toronto, Canada.

AMERICAN GROWING PAINS

5

While soccer captivated people around the world, the sport experienced problems gaining popularity in the United States, where other sports grabbed the lion's share of interest. In spite of these problems, progress has been made in developing American soccer.

As early as 1657 a Boston law attacked soccer. Responding to angry citizens, the law stated that "Forasmuch as sundry complaints are made that several persons have received hurt by boys and young men playing at foot-ball in the streets," a fine of 20 shillings would be imposed on anyone participating in such an endeavor.

The sport failed to disappear, however. In 1820 Princeton students engaged in a kicking game they called "ballown," and seven years later Harvard students began their "Bloody Monday" tradition, an annual match between the freshman and sophomore classes that normally dissolved into a lengthy brawl. Harvard authorities eventually banned the controversial event.

By the 1860s Boston high schools were playing soccer on the Boston Common, and the first American soccer club, the Oneida Football Club of Boston, appeared about the same time. The sport spread to other eastern cities, where large numbers of European immigrants lived, and to St. Louis, Missouri, which developed into the hotbed of American soccer. However, a variation of soccer, in which the player could carry the

Interest in soccer in America got a big boost when Pelé brought his winning performance and personality to the U.S. He waves to the crowd in his debut with the New York Cosmos in 1975.

ball as well as kick it, gained more popularity around the nation. This version gradually evolved into American football.

In 1884 a group of soccer enthusiasts met in New Jersey to discuss the formation of a league. Though short-lived, the American Football Association at least started what would become an organized American institution. Two years later an all-star squad from the American Football Association played the nation's first international game when they met Canada for a three-game exhibition series. The sport received another boost in 1904 when a British soccer team called the Pilgrims, including the best players from England's top amateur clubs, traveled around the United States in a series of exhibition games against American teams. The English amateurs showed how long United States soccer still had to go by posting a 21–2 record.

American soccer received a needed push on June 21, 1913, with the establishment of the United States Football Association (it changed to the United States Soccer Football Association in 1945). Behind the guiding spirit of Thomas Cahill, the organization attempted to make soccer "the national pastime of the winter in this country." The USFA realized they faced an uphill battle, but they charged into the fray with raised hopes.

A series of actions followed. The inaugural National Challenge Cup, the country's first national soccer championship, was held the same year. Nine years later came the National Amateur Cup, only one year after the formation of America's initial professional soccer league, the American Soccer League. Comprising mainly

East Coast teams that relied upon Scottish players, the league struggled until the decade's end when it collapsed in the face of the Great Depression.

A handful of American players gained praise for their play. Tops among them was the inside forward, Billy Gonsalves. One observer stated that in the 1920s and 1930s, Gonsalves was "probably the best player of the period." A large man, Gonsalves could kick a ball with such force that he frequently scored from long distances. A member of the Soccer Hall of Fame claimed that nobody outperformed Gonsalves. "When we speak of the greatest American player of all time, we think of Billy Gonsalves. He was a legend. For six years in a row he played with five different teams that

Soccer has been played on schoolyards and neighborhood playgrounds for generations, but the professional game has not caught on in the United States as it has in Europe and South America.

A history of brawling and rioting by soccer fans in Europe and South America is one factor that turned American audiences away from the professional sport. Here police wield cudgels to subdue unruly fans during an Italian major league game in Bologna. Outbursts of violence occur before, during, and after games.

won the Challenge Cup. He played for the World Cup team in 1930 and 1934. He was the best."

The main problem with soccer's attempt to gain a foothold in the United States was that most of the players were foreign or recent immigrants. Americans had a difficult time relating to a game dominated by strange-sounding names. They preferred homebred games like baseball and football.

Americans shied away from the violence that seemed to be so much a part of each match.

Newspaper headlines, such as the one that appeared in the *New York Times* on April 20, 1927, reporting "FOUR HURT IN RIOT AT SOCCER GAME," did little to help the sport's image.

The most serious attempts to organize an American professional league arose in 1967, when both the United Soccer Association (USA) and the National Professional Soccer League (NPSL) fielded teams. After experiencing difficulty attracting spectators—only 648 fans watched Detroit battle Boston—the two leagues merged in early 1968 into the North American Soccer League (NASL) of 17 teams.

Though it landed a television contract, the league lost so much money that only five franchises remained to play the next year. Three additional franchises were added by 1971. The following year the league implemented a college draft and passed a rule requiring that each team include on its roster at least two American or Canadian players. But the moves did not improve fan support; the mandatory American players normally sat on the bench in favor of the more talented foreign stars.

The sole move that brought attention to American soccer, ironically, rested upon the enormously gifted shoulders of a foreign athlete—Pelé. Though near the end of a fabulous career, the Brazilian superstar readily accepted the offer to play for the New York Cosmos. He explained at the time, "If an offer came from any other country, I would turn it down. But to play in the United States is different. I love soccer. I've been playing around the world for 20 years. Why should I not come to the United States and try to help the game?"

U.S. professional soccer leagues were dominated by foreign players until Kyle Rote Jr. (left), son of a professional football star, led the NASL in scoring in 1973. At one time the league had 20 teams, but it folded in 1984.

Before his first game with the Cosmos, Pelé told the press, "Everyone in life has a mission, and my dream is that one day the United States will know soccer like the rest of the world." On June 15, 1975, before a national television audience and triple the normal attendance in the stands, Pelé scored a goal in the game that, his fans hoped, would help jump-start soccer's future in the country.

Huge crowds showed up whenever Pelé was in town. The popular athlete appeared on television to promote soccer, showed President Gerald Ford how to kick a soccer ball, and spoke at youth gatherings. As a result of his efforts and appeal, more young people took to the soccer fields. One expert claimed that while in the mid-1960s only 50,000 American boys and girls played soccer, because of Pelé the number soon soared to 600,000.

The NASL provided American professionals a chance to gain worldwide recognition. Two such stars were Kyle Rote Jr. and Al Trost. They succeeded in a league dominated by foreign players and, as such, helped popularize soccer in the United States.

Born in Dallas, Texas, on Christmas Day, 1950, Kyle Rote Jr. had a tough act to follow in the sporting world. His father, Kyle Sr., earned All-American football honors at Southern Methodist University, then starred with the professional New York Giants.

Kyle starred in three sports during high school. According to writer Bill Gutman, Rote and some friends started kicking a football around a field soccer-style to get in shape. One day an English sportswriter named Ron Griffith offered a few tips. It was the start of Rote's soccer career.

After one year at Oklahoma State University, Rote transferred to the University of the South in Tennessee. He joined the school's soccer team and soon excelled. In 1971 he set school records with 17 goals and 7 assists in only 12 games.

Though he had no plans to pursue a sports career after graduation, Rote was the first player selected by the Dallas Tornado of the NASL in 1972. After a year spent in learning the game sufficiently to compete with the

European stars who flocked to the new league, Rote became the first American to lead the league in scoring in 1973 when he edged Trinidad native Warren Archibald of Miami by one point. Rote received the Rookie of the Year award for his play.

The following years reflected his star status. In addition to leading his team to a second division title in 1977, Rote starred for the United States National team 1973–1975.

Born in St. Louis on February 7, 1949, Al Trost turned to soccer as a youth because of his small size. In addition, he claimed he liked soccer "because everyone could be involved. You didn't need a lot of equipment, just someone to have a ball."

After a fine high school soccer career, Trost selected St. Louis University because of its renowned soccer program. During his three years at the school, his team lost only once. St. Louis won the NCAA soccer championship in both 1969 and 1970, and Trost twice received his sport's highest honor, the Hermann Award for top college soccer player.

Trost starred for the 1972 Olympic team, and in 1973 helped the United States National team defeat heavily favored Poland, 1–0, when he rocketed a 20-yard shot by the Polish goalkeeper.

For a time, the NASL prospered. The league expanded to 20 teams and imported other famous foreign stars such as Gordon Banks, Eusebio, and Giorgio Chinaglia. However, subsequent financial problems due to lagging attendance hounded the NASL. The league's demise was only a matter of time when the national television contract was not renewed for the 1982 season. Though the NASL struggled through three more seasons, it folded after the 1984 schedule.

The chief difference separating the NASL from previous failed efforts to promote soccer was its success in implanting the sport among America's youth. Today more boys and girls play soccer in the United States than any other sport except basketball. Even though Pelé could not save professional soccer in America, he introduced the game to an entire generation of enthusiasts. As one writer suggested of young America, "These players are the future of soccer in North America. Pelé's example, both on and off the field, has been one of the factors in their love of the game."

6

THEY MAKE MAGIC

Soccer has produced many stars in its lengthy history. With its incredible popularity around the world, these individuals received widespread acclaim for the wizardry they displayed on the field.

In American soccer, no name stands out like Alexi Lalas. Born Panayotis Alexander Lalas on June 1, 1970, in Michigan, Lalas moved to Greece with his father at age 6 when his parents divorced. There he joined soccer clubs and developed a love for the game.

In 1980 Lalas returned to Michigan, where he starred in both hockey and soccer for Cranbrook High School. When he helped lead his team to the 1987 high school state championship, Lalas was named Michigan's high school soccer player of the year.

Lalas attended Rutgers University, at first joining both the hockey and soccer teams. However, after his first year he dropped hockey so that he could focus solely on soccer. While captain of the team in 1991, Lalas captured the sport's highest collegiate honor for soccer— the Hermann Trophy. Lalas also played for the 1991 U.S. team that won the gold medal in the Pan-American games, and for the 1992 Olympic team.

Two tough years plagued Lalas following the Olympics, partly because of a broken foot. He attempted to play in Europe, but his poor

Born in Michigan, Alexi Lalas (22) starred in high school and at Rutgers University. After helping the U.S. team to a first-round win in the 1994 World Cup, he became the first American to be signed by an Italian major league team.

performances left him on the sidelines. He again headed back to the United States, regained his form with arduous practices and hard work, and helped the 1994 World Cup team to an impressive showing. The United States team, though not expected to do well, advanced to the tournament's second round by upsetting Colombia, 2–1.

Though they subsequently lost to Brazil, 1–0, Lalas's outstanding play won rave notices. He explained to a newspaper reporter that he succeeded because "the key is to recognize your abilities and not overextend yourself. I work hard to clog the middle, to mark my man, to clear out to those people who have more ability."

The 1994 World Cup earned Lalas a second look from European teams. German, English, and Italian offers landed in his lap, and when Lalas signed with Padua, he became the first American to play in Italy's premier league, which many observers claim is the best in the world.

Fan reaction stunned the outgoing Lalas. When he arrived at Venice's Marco Polo airport, a large crowd enthusiastically greeted the American. "That's not the welcome you'd get in the States," stated Lalas to *Newsweek* magazine. "As an American soccer player you're always on the quest for recognition."

One facet marked Lalas's soccer career— determination. He advanced to top-caliber soccer even though he lacked the offensive weaponry of some of his colleagues. As he told one reporter, "Through my career, people have said there's no way you can play on the Olympic team, there's no way you can play on the national team, there's no way you can play in the World Cup and have success. But you know, here I am."

Another American soccer player enjoyed more success than Lalas and played for the first World Cup championship team produced by the United States. Born on February 1, 1966, in California, Michelle Akers earned All-American status three times in high school before attending the University of Central Florida. A four-time collegiate All-American, Akers captured the Hermann Trophy as top player in the nation.

A member of the U.S. Women's National team since 1985, Akers watched women's soccer go through an incredible transformation. When she first traveled to Italy with the women's team in 1985, the difference in the two squads startled the athlete. "We didn't look like a national team," she mentioned to *Sports Illustrated* magazine. "All we had were these lime-green and purple uniforms. No one was fit. We were just a bunch of kids, we didn't know what we were getting into."

Sporting a shot so powerful that one of her coaches gushed, "They feel like cannonballs when you catch them," Akers put on a dazzling performance during the 1991 Women's World Cup tournament held in China. She scored more goals than anyone else in the competition to help her team win its first five games and land a spot in the final against Norway.

With the Final tied, 1–1, and less than three minutes remaining, Akers chased down a long pass that landed within 20 yards of the Norwegian goal. A Norwegian defender reached the ball and started to nudge it back toward her goaltender just as Akers arrived. The

A two-time Female Athlete of the Year, Michelle Akers scored the winning goal in this game against Norway to bring the Women's World Cup championship to the United States for the first time in 1991.

American shoved the defender out of the way, sped after and intercepted the backward pass, steered the ball to the left of the onrushing goalie, and smacked it into the net for the winning goal. For the first time in the 20th century, a team from the United States owned a World Cup championship. For her stellar play in this and other tournaments, Akers was named Female Athlete of the Year in both 1990 and 1991.

Three years later Akers was diagnosed with Epstein-Barr virus, more commonly known as chronic fatigue syndrome. The disease sapped every ounce of strength and forced Akers to miss entire games. As she explained, "When it was bad, I couldn't sit up in a chair. All I could do was lie in bed. At night I sweated so much I went through two or three T-shirts."

To help her condition, Akers altered the hectic pace of her life and placed more emphasis upon family and religion. She learned to play only as many minutes as her body allowed, which usually meant about one half of each game, and developed a more patient style of play, in which she conserved her energy for offensive bursts. Even with the limitation, Akers remained the most feared offensive threat in women's soccer, averaging a goal a game.

Akers' other major interest was the development of soccer in the United States, which she believes is on a proper course. "To keep hearing people put down American soccer is really frustrating—and tees me off," she asserted. With more players like Akers, she will not have to worry about criticism for long.

The most recognized athlete in the world in the 1980s was soccer's Maradona. Born in devastating poverty on October 30, 1960, in Buenos Aires, Argentina, Diego Armand Maradona rarely walked around town without a soccer ball as a youth. He practiced with it, slept with it, kicked it, and learned so many nuances of dribbling and passing that he guided his youth team, Los Cebollitos, to 140 straight victories.

The youngster, wearing #10 to honor his idol Pelé, soon gained legendary status in

Argentina, even putting on demonstrations of his soccer prowess at halftime exhibitions of professional matches when he was only 10 years old. Before he turned 16, Maradona starred for the Argentinos Juniors, scoring 43 goals in 1980 and gaining the attention of one of the nation's top junior clubs, the Boca Juniors. When he led the Boca Juniors to a national title, the *London Sunday Times* announced, "About once in 20 years, a footballer of genius emerges. The last was Pelé, the great Brazilian player. Now there is another—Diego Maradona of Argentina."

Not all was rosy for the young athlete. Though playing for Argentina's national team at 16, Maradona suffered what he viewed as a humiliation by being cut shortly before the 1978 World Cup because his coach feared the pressure would be too great for the youngster. When Argentina succeeded in capturing the World Cup, Maradona felt more miserable and refused to speak to the coach for six months.

Though Maradona played poorly in the 1982 World Cup, he returned with a vengeance in 1986. Called "Maradona's Cup" for the dominating play he exhibited, Maradona scored every Argentine goal in the quarterfinal and semifinal wins, and notched five goals in seven games to garner the tournament's Most Valuable Player award.

In the quarterfinals, he tallied both goals against England in a 2–1 win. His second goal stunned onlookers as he deftly dribbled by English defenders, faked the goaltender into committing one way, then changed directions and planted the ball into the net. One reporter wrote of the goal that "there was no denying

As a youth in Argentina, Diego Maradona idolized Pelé. He became his own country's idol in the 1980s, winning the MVP award by leading his team to the 1986 World Cup championship.

the brilliance of Maradona's second goal. Collecting the ball in his own half, he waltzed past the English defenders for a truly amazing solo goal." According to another, Maradona "changed gears like a fantastic sports car. It was unbelievable. The ball looked like it was glued to his feet."

After scoring both goals in a 2–0 semifinal win over Belgium and the only goal in a semifinal tie with Italy, 1–1, Maradona aced the championship for Argentina against West

Germany when he nudged a fantastic pass through four West German defenders to teammate Jorge Burruchaga, who veered it into the goal for the 3–2 win.

Though Maradona experienced harsher days in the 1990s, mainly because of his problems with drugs, fans remembered his unequaled talent for scoring crucial goals.

Roberto Baggio carried a dream with him from his youth in Caldogno, Italy. "Every day growing up I had this dream about the World Cup," he explained to *Newsweek* magazine. "I score the winning goal."

Italian major leaguer Roberto Baggio (10) has been called "soccer's Michael Jordan." Soccer coaches named him the world's best player in 1993.

Born in 1967, Baggio first played Italian soccer in 1982. A potent right foot and blinding speed on the field led other athletes to exclaim that Baggio is "a player who makes magic." Nicknames indicate the high level of fame Baggio has achieved. He has been called "The Phenomenon," "The Living Wonder," and "soccer's Michael Jordan." Fans in Florence, Italy, so loved Baggio that when the team sold him to Turin in 1990, they rioted in anger.

In 1993 Baggio captured two of soccer's highest honors. Journalists named him the top European player, and soccer coaches selected Baggio as the world's premier player. A quiet man who prefers to stay home with his wife and children, Baggio illustrates that great athleticism and humility can create a forceful combination.

WE NEED THEM
TOO MUCH

7

A Brazilian sportswriter once tried to explain what soccer meant to the people of his nation. "Soccer is everything to Brazilians," he wrote. "For a lot, it's the only thing. People live and die by the sport, not just at the pro level but in the sandlots as well. In the United States and Europe people have other ways of affirming themselves as people. In Brazil it is not like that."

Though soccer has had a rough trial in the United States, inroads have been made in recent years that provide more than a glimmer of hope. Even one of soccer's failures—the collapse of the NASL—yielded positive results among youth because of its promotional activities. As its main attraction, Pelé, explained, "The NASL had planted seeds everywhere, and the sport was now delighting kids—boys and girls—all over this huge country. In the ten years since the death of the league, the sport has gone on growing irresistibly at the youth level."

The American Youth Soccer Organization (AYSO), which started in California in 1964, particularly benefitted from the NASL. Building upon the philosophy that every boy and girl plays at least half of each game, the AYSO operates different divisions for young people ranging from ages five to 18. At first plagued by the problem of who would coach the youths who poured into the organization, the AYSO overcame the issue with a series of coaching schools that turned out knowledgeable adults.

Ronaldo (center) is the latest star to come out of Brazil. Playing for Internationale of Milan, the 21-year-old striker was named FIFA World Player of the Year in 1997 for the second straight year.

The results were phenomenal. Starting with 9 teams in 1964, the AYSO had organized 9,000 teams of 165,000 players in 21 states by 1978. Eleven years later the numbers had rocketed to a half million boys and girls joining 24,000 teams in 36 states, Washington, D.C., and Puerto Rico. City parks and recreation departments, soccer clubs, and community groups such as the YMCA and YWCA supplemented these numbers with their own popular programs. These figures allowed AYSO personnel to boast, "There is no limit to the growth in sight."

Jenny Peters, a 14-year-old Michigan AYSO soccer player, was typical of the thousands of youths to take up the game. "I like soccer because it is a fast-paced game that has a lot of action. You have to use your feet and be good at skills that other sports don't have."

When Paul Caligiuri, a former AYSO member, scored the goal that put the United States National team into the 1990 World Cup, it vindicated all the efforts made by hundreds of coaches and sponsors throughout the nation. AYSO had come of age in the world of soccer.

One result of the successful AYSO programs was that as younger kids advanced into high school, they put pressure upon their schools to institute varsity soccer. Because of its lower costs, most high schools readily agreed.

However, high schools experienced their own problems. One school superintendent recalled that in the early 1970s only 14 boys tried out for the varsity squad, and they were "mostly the rejects of the football program." A few years later more than 70 boys appeared for varsity soccer.

American soccer flourished at the collegiate level as well. College soccer began in 1905 when a group of eastern universities formed the Intercollegiate Association Football League, which became the Intercollegiate Soccer Football Association in 1925. Containing differences from regular soccer, such as playing four quarters rather than two halves, and allowing substitutes, college soccer grew slowly until the 1960s, when the sport caught on. The previous year the NCAA had started its first national championship for soccer, a move which offered to high school soccer players the

Women's soccer has attained World Cup and Olympic stature equal to men's. Here Shannon MacMillan scores a goal against China in the 1996 Olympics.

same opportunity that football, baseball, and basketball athletes had—the chance to play their sport and earn a championship while in college. Consequently, by 1984, more college soccer teams existed than football squads.

Soccer's extraordinary growth spread to women's programs in the 1970s. The National Women's Soccer Association (NWSA) was formed in 1977, and by 1993 more than five million women were registered. One official stated that women's soccer is "the fastest growing NCAA team sport. Because of the growing popularity of soccer, it definitely has a chance to be the number one women's collegiate sport."

Acting as the chief guardian of soccer in the United States from its headquarters in Colorado Springs, Colorado, the United States Soccer Federation (USSF) managed 11 different national cup competitions for different ages, sponsored educational programs, enforced uniformity of rules, and settled disputes among clubs. It also assembled and trained the U.S. National team that played in the World Cup and other international tournaments.

A major boost to American soccer occurred in 1994 when the United States hosted the World Cup. Thousands of spectators who would not normally be exposed to the game flocked to stadiums in cities like Chicago, Detroit, Los Angeles, Boston, and San Francisco to watch the best players compete in the sport's premier event. Professional soccer benefitted when the U.S. team surprised the experts with a solid showing. Buoyed by the positive response from fans, an organization called Major League Soccer went ahead with its plans to begin play in 1995 with 12 teams.

The outlook for soccer in America appeared more optimistic in the 1990s than at any time in the sport's history.

As the legendary Pelé admonished an audience one day, "Pay attention to the young of the world, the children. We need them too much."

CHRONOLOGY

1697 B.C.	The Chinese emperor, Huang-Ti, starts tsu-chu.
A.D. 43–407	Roman legionnaires bring harpastum to England.
1175	The English game ludus pilae is mentioned in writing.
April 13, 1314	King Edward II bans football.
1389	Richard II bans football and tennis.
1457	James III of Scotland bans football and golf.
1572	Queen Elizabeth bans football in London.
1820	Princeton students first play "ballown."
1827	Harvard students start their "Bloody Monday" games.
Dec. 8, 1863	London Football Association issues the Laws of the London Football Association.
1871	First Challenge Cup tournament is held in England.
1872	First international game is held when England plays Scotland.
1888	The world's first professional soccer league, the Professional League, forms.
1904	The Federation Internationale de Football Association (FIFA) is organized.
	The Pilgrims, a British soccer team, travel the United States in a series of exhibition matches.
1905	The Intercollegiate Association Football League is formed in the United States.
June 21, 1913	The United States Football Association organizes.
1930	The first World Cup tournament is held.
1959	The first NCAA soccer championship tournament is held in the United States.
1964	The American Youth Soccer Organization (AYSO) is formed in California.
1968	The North American Soccer League (NASL) is formed.
1977	The National Women's Soccer Association (NWSA) is formed in the United States.
1984	The NASL folds.
1991	The United States Women's National team wins the World Cup.
1994	The United States hosts the World Cup.

FURTHER READING

Arnold, Caroline. *Soccer: From Neighborhood Play to the World Cup*. New
    York: Franklin Watts, 1991.

Gardner, Paul. *The Simplest Game*. New York: Macmillan Publishing Company,
    1994.

Gutman, Bill. *Modern Soccer Superstars*. New York: Dodd, Mead &
    Company, 1979.

Howard, Dale E. *Soccer Stars*. Chicago: Childrens Press, 1994.

Kowet, Don. *Pelé*. New York: Atheneum, 1976.

LaBlanc, Michael L. and Richard Henshaw. *The World Encyclopedia of Soccer*.
    Detroit: Visible Ink Press, 1994.

Phillips, Glen and Tim Oldham. *World Cup USA '94*. New York:
    Harper Paperbacks, 1994.

Rote, Kyle Jr. with Basil Kane. *Kyle Rote Jr.'s Complete Book of Soccer*.
    New York: Simon and Schuster, 1978.

Yannis, Alex. *Inside Soccer*. New York: McGraw-Hill Book Company, 1980.

WORLD CUP FINALS

YEAR	SCORE		HOST COUNTRY
1930	Uruguay	4	
	Argentina	2	Uruguay
1934	Italy	2	
	Czechoslovakia	1	Italy
1938	Italy	4	
	Hungary	2	France
1950	Uruguay	2	
	Brazil	1	Brazil
1954	West Germany	3	
	Hungary	2	Switzerland
1958	Brazil	5	
	Sweden	2	Sweden
1962	Brazil	3	
	Czechoslovakia	1	Chile
1966	England	4	
	West Germany	2	England
1970	Brazil	4	
	Italy	1	Mexico
1974	West Germany	2	
	Holland	1	Argentina
1982	Italy	3	
	West Germany	1	Spain
1986	Argentina	3	
	West Germany	2	Mexico
1990	West Germany	1	
	Argentina	0	Italy
1994	Brazil	0	
	Italy	0	United States
	(Brazil wins shoot-out, 3–2)		

INDEX

JOHN F. WUKOVITS is a teacher and writer from Trenton, Michigan. His work has appeared in more than 25 national publications, including *Sports History* magazine. His books include a biography of the World War II commander Admiral Clifton Sprague, and he has written biographies of Barry Sanders, Vince Lombardi, John Stockton, and Jack Nicklaus for Chelsea House. A graduate of the University of Notre Dame, Wukovits is the father of three daughters—Amy, Julie, and Karen.